spot

PETS

BIRDS

by Mari Schuh

AMICUS | AMICUS INK

beak

feathers

Look for these
words and pictures
as you read.

perch

claws

Chirp! Chirp!
A pet bird is happy to see you!

Look at the cage.
It is the bird's home.
It has food, water, and toys.

Do you see the beak?
It opens nuts and seeds.
It helps the bird climb.

beak

feathers

Do you see the feathers?
A bird cleans them with its beak.
They are soft and bright.

Do you see the perch?
It is made of wood.
A bird stands here.

perch

Do you see the claws?
Each foot has four claws.
They hold on tight.

claws

A bird visits its owner.
Then it flies around.
Chirp, chirp!

Do you see the beak?
It opens nuts and seeds.
It helps the bird climb.

beak

feathers

Do you see the feathers?
A bird cleans them with its beak.
They are soft and bright.

beak

feathers

Did you find?

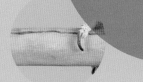

perch

claws

Do you see the perch?
It is made of wood.
A bird stands here.

perch

Do you see the claws?
Each foot has four claws.
They hold on tight.

claws

Spot is published by Amicus and Amicus Ink
P.O. Box 1329, Mankato, MN 56002
www.amicuspublishing.us

Library of Congress Cataloging-in-Publication Data
Names: Schuh, Mari C., 1975- author.
Title: Birds / by Mari Schuh.
Description: Mankato, MN : Amicus/Amicus Ink, [2019] |
Series: Spot. Pets | Audience: K to grade 3.
Identifiers: LCCN 2017024593 (print) | LCCN 2017030610
   (ebook) | ISBN 9781681514468 (pdf) |
   ISBN 9781681513645 (library bound) |
   ISBN 9781681522845 (paperback)
Subjects: LCSH: Cage birds--Juvenile literature. | Cage
   birds--Behavior--Juvenile literature. | CYAC: Birds as pets.
Classification: LCC SF461 (ebook) | LCC SF461 .S38 2019
   (print) | DDC 636.6/8--dc23
LC record available at https://lccn.loc.gov/2017024593

Printed in China

HC 10 9 8 7 6 5 4 3 2 1
PB 10 9 8 7 6 5 4 3 2 1

Wendy Dieker, editor
Deb Miner, series designer
Ciara Beitlich, book designer
Holly Young, photo researcher

Photos by Alamy 8–9, 10–11;
Dreamstime 6–7, iStock 3, 12–13, 14;
Shutterstock cover, 1, 4–5

BIRDS